LOREN KLEINMAN

Breakable Things

Winter Goose
Publishing

Winter Goose Publishing
2701 Del Paso Road, 130-92
Sacramento, CA 95835

www.wintergoosepublishing.com
Contact Information: info@wintergoosepublishing.com

Breakable Things

COPYRIGHT © 2015 by Loren Kleinman

First Edition, March 2015

Cover Art by Winter Goose Publishing
Photograph "True To Form" by Fred Fleisher
fredfleisher.net
Typesetting by Odyssy Books

ISBN: 978-1-941058-25-1

Published in the United States of America

Table of Contents

"There is a crack in everything.
That's how the light gets in."

—Leonard Cohen, "Anthem"

For Claudia, Joseph, Jenny, and Kyle

Breakable Things

My kitchen
is the only thing that exists,

one room,
floating up
above New Jersey's fault lines.

All the things it holds
within its walls
float around me
while I sit at the glass table,
on the wicker chair,
drinking a glass of wine.

The ceiling is its own solar system.

The lights circle
around me like planets
and orbit around my cat.

Day after day,
I sit in my kitchen,
eating, smoking, drinking
alone.

I am the only girl in the world
hiding in cabinets
next to the breakable things.

Love Poem

On a Tuesday night,
I get lost
in a love poem by Bukowski.

I want to be held
and loved
by someone with big arms,
with ears and feet,
just like me.

I think of all the men,
all of them,
their hands holding me
like the women held Bukowski
in the love poem he wrote.

Only he's him
and I'm me
and he's dead
and I'm on a bed
on a fancy silver sheet,
legs crossed,
eyes scrambling
over the words
love love love

and I can't get out of those words,
that remind me of men loving me
and me loving some of them,

and others not,
and them wanting me
to love them back
but I couldn't.

Those lines of the poem fill me up
and make me glow
like a hot doorknob

and I want Bukowski
to take the book from me,
tell me to not read another word
or he'll smother me with paper,
drench me in wine
and lighter fluid
and strike a match.

Joe Is Full of Faults and Green Grass

Even when he gets fucked up
and comes to me in the chair
from Manhattan at sunrise,
I still love him.

I know I can kiss him,
make the sights of his past
become petunias
and linen
in his belly button.

He lets me hold him,
his eyes like the Great Lakes.

In the middle of the kitchen,
the coffee press full,
piles of laundry and pain
on the floor,
and the window, open,

wind all over us.

The Heart Is Not a Box

It doesn't hold chocolates,
nor is it heart-shaped,
or red.

It doesn't have an arrow
through its center.

The heart is an empty place,
a desolate parking lot,

or the windy sky,
wide open.

The Past Is a Full Room

Just talk about the dead,
and they appear.

Talk about love
and you fall into it, head first.

The shelves are a touch screen
for anything you want:
cappuccino, a glass of wine,
or a biscuit.

Listen to the pencils
put themselves back
in their cups.

The chairs push back
under the desk.

The windows close
and wrap the walls
in their glass.

The paper is unmarked.
The lines move under your pencil
as you write.

No one loses anything here.

Past Love

I wish I could've hiked the Appalachian Trail with you
so we could feel lost and found together,

but the phone died
and we couldn't find each other back then.

Life is very much the same,
hotel rooms,
cheeseburger and fries,
and our bodies.

If we walked together on the rocky precipice,
we'd fill all the empty rooms in the forest
or at least the emptiness beneath us.

But pain breaks the man.
Pain breaks the woman.
And I couldn't get there in time
to cover your eyes from the gun
and the head.

The more I think of you,
the more I realize
I've already dreamed of you for years.
Someone already wrote a book about us
and someone else already made the movie.

This is how it works:
you make an engagement ring out of a straw wrapper

and propose to me
in the diner at six a.m. in Manhattan
as the sun comes up,

and you hold my face in your palms
under the dim, cracked light,
out of that dark hell you call your home
and tell me you're in love with me
despite the rotten skin of your past

and you're going to go down on me
whether I like it or not
in your flight suit
for the next eight hundred years.

When I Was a Little Girl

I was pigtailed,
running through high grass,
no sexual adventure
between my thighs.

A man loved me,
he loved me so.

When I was a little girl,
he took me on rides
in a long car,
on an interstate far off
to another town.

His wet tongue showered me
and fingered out the child.

He cut me
and bruised my wrists
with soft breath.

He was a man
inside the light.

I ran past him
on the school ground,
and he blew me a kiss.

I didn't care to love another.

That Time You Took LSD
Under the Bridge

You were once a dinosaur
hiking up Mount Everest
before it was Mount Everest.

You fell from its side
and landed in the ocean
kicking up bubbles

and turned into a snail,

then, a human being,

and bumped into a continent,
rose from the water
and floated on waves,
eyes toward the sun,

the sun no longer the sun,
but a round yellow ball
that turned into an orange,

and you squeezed its juice,
held your mouth open,

eyes closed,
head shaking,
free.

Sky Breasts

The silence takes me
to another dream
where I'm young and blind.

I have nothing left to give
to the child on the corner,
the one that holds out
the cup for pennies.

Mamma, can you hear me?

I'm here,
behind the skin shutters
that cover my sky breasts.

See me stand
on the broken road
under the pavement.

There's a world no one knows,

the one that lives
inside my fingers.

Mother Falls from the Sky

Her wings flap
like feathered fingers
at every leaf,
every bark shank, every
pointed branch.

She dives head first,
beak spearheaded
into the grassy floor.

Each bone rattles
like a mariachi band
shaking the last maraca,

the sound of cracking,
shattering the small windows
of my life.

She wakes from the dead,
opens her eyes wide
and turns her head

to hear the chirps
somewhere up there:

the chicks she watched
hatching,

their last sound
for her on earth.

Goodbye, Pickle

Her fur spread through
the flattened ground
like a Chinese fan.

On top of the small grave,
I leave catnip,
a paper clip,
and a rubber mouse.

I press my hand
into the dirt
so she'll feel I was there.

The air is cold,
all the air blowing
in and around me.

I tighten my winter coat
and press my back to the tree.

I close my eyes,
imagine her four legs
flapping behind.

Joanne Makes Snow Angels in Summer

On the lawn in the backyard,
Joanne makes snow angels
in the middle of summer.

She flaps her arms hard
and the tall grass gets flattened
as she grabs it,
palms flat against the dirt.

She plucks strands of green hair
in large handfuls
and throws them like confetti.

They fall on her as she sings
Snow angel, snow angel,
I'm making fucking snow angels
and she's laughing
and I'm not laughing
and she's bleeding on her right knee.

Joanne lies there,
the empty bottle of wine
next to her
like a Buddha in a parka,

and all I can do is watch,
not try to help her,
but watch,

then go to the bottle,
hold it,
bring it to my lips,
and suck venom.

Books Are Left for Dead

Like coke-binged whores
on city streets,
books are left for dead.

They want to be touched.

Make love to them with your fingers,
coddle them in your palms,
their flat-chested front covers
gripping you closer.

Sometimes they are stacked,
church candles
that blur and dim the dark.

And all those words,
how you sneak them away
in the back of used car lots,
in dressing rooms,
cracking the spines,
turning their insides,
giving in to the addiction.

We want to keep reading.

We hold out our arms
and let the words find
a beating vein.

Chipped Wine Glass

She stands tall,
a stem.

Her roots
go underground,
deep into the dirt.

Cylinder legs,
a laugh caught in the circular whirl,
an echo in the clear bubble.

Behind her,
a concert plays
in A minor.

She feels like a fool,
alone and full of wine.

The world doesn't listen
to drunk women.

She is a glass,
full of the things
she hates,

chipped in the light.

Ordinary Things

A half-mile up, there's a rest stop.

Three miles west,
the road bends at Pinebrook and Davenson.

Four miles east,
the highest point of a mountain
touches the sky
with its white top

and a woman in a hair net wakes up
from her hotel bed and walks
to the bathroom
to brush her teeth.

A dog barks next door.
Inside, a cat scratches
the posts of the bed frame.

In the kitchen next to the house,
someone scrambles eggs
and toasts bread.

The boy texts his girlfriend from the couch.

Outside, the street is cracked
at the edge of the sidewalk.

The newspaper sits in the mailbox,
wrapped in plastic
covered with dew.

You drive through
and look up
at the flock of symmetrical birds
flying overhead,

back at the sign that says
next rest stop 60 miles,

back at the curve
of the steering wheel,
at your hands,
and the road ahead,

wondering how
you got here after all.

Everything Is Better in Disorder

At the edge of Chelsea and Hell,
I turn to the bartender
and ask for another Merlot.

In my mind, I drive off
and dance in a dark club.

I think of what Italy looks like,
or the glow of traffic
in a rearview mirror.

I take off between now
and later tonight.

Mark sits across from me:
a burnt up engine,
a barrel of supplies,
a cart of groceries
in a full line.

He says I don't understand
the art of banter.

I watch him,
two feet away from me,

and would rather screw.

He Breaks Me Like a Glass Plate

I'm cut on the floor,
porcelain in the skin,
and he breaks
he breaks he breaks he breaks me,
like I'm a plate on the counter top,
his hands, tired of me,
let me go towards the tile
and he's willing to crush me,
to step to step to step on me
the not-so-soft part of the skull,
the part that cracks when stepped on,
shatters like an exploded vein.

I was just sitting there,
waiting for him to come home,
and the days kept changing,
the sound of them turning is loud and hurts
and I wait,
my back against a mattress.

I wish I was someone else,
the moon,
younger
and bloodless,
more loveable and perfect,
less breakable.

Last night I dreamt
he came home and slipped

back into the bed he'd left me in for days.
I forgave him for calling me a slut,
for shattering the love I had for myself,
for killing me with a kitchen knife,
for doubting my love for him,
and not calling me for days.

My heart is tired.

I'm so tired,
so tired.

I'm so tired,
I wish I was the moon tonight.

First-Date Oysters

You're buttering my crackers
and pouring me Prosecco

and I'm letting you do this,
allowing you to feed me,
attempting to fill
my hollowness.

I scoop the slippery bodies
from the cool shucked shells
and dip them into the
cocktail sauce.

Smiling,
you watch me chew.

Death takes the shape
of an oyster tonight.
I swallow it.

We stare at the plate,
killing them off
one by one.

We hold hands
and do not mourn.

Oysters are an aphrodisiac
you remind me.

And I feel nothing,
just the feeling
of wanting
to feel something.

It's the same date as before,
a dream.

Even the oysters,
they are alive somewhere,
dancing in their shells
far away from the mouths
of lonely people.

After You Cheat on Me
the Light Is Still On

You fuck up beyond recognition when you can't see me
in the light, when you can't see
my eyes shine from the tears.

You hurt the people you love the most. You leave the
light on so I can see the anger and hurt, so I can see
your dead mother, your abusive father, and your son
swimming in Georgia.
You burn your darkest life onto me and then kiss me,
your charred baby.

Under the light, I still love you. I can see you. I can see
all of you. All the broken parts, the missing ones, the
parts you don't even want to see, like how you still love
your ex, how you broke your favorite J mug, the lost ID
on a train somewhere, or how you broke my heart in five
different places, then tried to glue them back together.

Now we're vulnerable and terrified. We'd rather choose
the dark. We'd rather wrap ourselves in the deep sighs
of our lungs and in our messy bed and condom wrap-
pers and tequila.

Just to get back at you, I die a little. Just to get back. I
cut into my thigh a little with your pocket knife. When
I cut the skin, when I cut it deep, the light passes
through, and me and you pass through with the sounds
of orgasms and happiness.

Erotica Story

I hold on to your waist,
lick your stomach
and suck on your fingers.

I lay your hand on my breasts
and put my head back
against the kitchen table.

I rock my waist
and you hold my hips as I rock.

You kiss me
and I kiss back.

Then I pull away
and you grab my hair,

pull me off the page,

and I fall, heavy,
on the purple couch
in your living room.

Spin the Bottle

We burn the last of the dime bag
tucked in my bra.

The kitchen is full of smoke
and friends.

Pasta sauce drips on the floor,
let the dog get it.

The plates stacked,
totem-like.

Pass the joint,
pour the tequila shot in my navel.

I kissed your best friend
with tongue.

You show the crowd your balls.
We're impressed.

In the End You Get Away

You blow the dandelion
and propel the seeds
to the ground.

The blanket is a ripped sheet of paper
over the dirt.

Under the dimmed sun,
we made love
like two lions.

Now you care as much as a dessert.

Stuck on Atlantic Between
3rd and Bond

The highway rings
like a tin drum.

There are wrecked people
all around me,
beautifully dressed in shame
and smoke.

I have a dime bag
and a forty-ounce.

With each sip, I wish
I was a piece of broken glass
for you to see
yourself in.

I wish I had clearer skin
and a cleaner smile.

I'm horny now
and want a man to fill me.

I want him to hold me so tight
that nothing broken will matter
any longer.

I want to inhale this anarchy,

the dusting of coke
on a marble table.

I want to forget about love,
all two hundred and twenty pounds of it,

chipped,
swimming
in antidepressants.

Kicked Back in a White
Honda Accord in NJ

We sat in our car,
feet kicked back over the hood
and watched the sun come up
from the bottom of New Jersey.

We watched the sun,
a big lightbulb
over the windshield.
It made us squint.

We held each other's hands
and smiled.

Our lips were cracked
from hours spent swimming.

The sky burned above us.

Lighting Up

We lit up together,
sucking in the bud
down and through our chests,
switching the pipe back
and forth,
and laughing
for the sake of being high.

Then, leaning into my face,
he lifted me up against the wall
and held me like a bong
and kissed the smoke out
of my deep mouth
and breathed it back
into his.

We made love on the kitchen floor,
the cold floor
with the lining of smoke
above us.

Two Weeks Ago I Would've Said
I Love You

He slides close to me
and drowns me in a long kiss.

We're in love again.

The city is cold
and snow hangs from our boots.

And we'll end up naked,
under the white sheet
of the city.

I Got Back from Maine and You Were Gone

Rather than cry,
I slept in your sweaty t-shirt and imagined
you against my skin,
you inside me
building a cabin
out of my rib cage
to hide in.

Now I smother my mouth
with your collar
and I smell you,
smell you
and the cologne I like so much,
the one that reminds me of you
and sadness and rotted wood.

I tear your shirt
and wrap it around my thighs
and hold myself
away from other men.

I cut out the sleeves
and put it around my neck
and tighten it
so I can't breathe

until my lips go cracked and blue
and the devil outside my door
can't kiss me.

I cling to the last strip
I cut out
and sew into my armpit,
the most tender body part
I saved for you,
once.

I try hard not to cry,
hold the knives and Valium
in my hand and cut
the rest of the cloth,
staple it to my mouth,

and laugh under my breath
because I'd never
have to talk to you
again.

We All Have to Go

I peed outside your door,
under your window,
on East 7th Street and Avenue B,

knees bent,
bare ass hovering
over the gum-stuck
sidewalk,
my back toward the trash cans,
and my head, a light bulb
on a string
you yanked on and off.

You laughed at me,
squatting there
across from Tompkins Square Park,
you drunker than me,
trying to explain how
we're all connected
in the universe.

Traditional

We got married in the isle
of the beer emporium
in China Town,

the cans stacked high around us
like the Great Wall.

We smelled of spilled booze,
sex,
and pork belly wonton.

We exchanged our beers like rings
and kissed,
empty cans on the floor.

General Instructions in Times of Disaster

We're in Japan—
typhoon season.

The wind
sticks into us,
its spears
in our sides
at Shibuya Crossing.
Torn rope
in my hands
wraps my palm like Okonomiyaki.

Hold on to me.

We Smile from Above
the Atmosphere

You hold my arms down,
take bites from my wrist,
swallow pieces of me.

I let you eat me whole
and lick the tight skin
that hangs from your teeth.

Where we speak,
the walls shake.

The sky changes.

Black blinds keep us from danger
and shroud the room in darkness.

We are the light in the sky,
the glue that binds
broken hearts.

We can't say no to our mouths,
to the pain we cause our bodies,
to pleasure.

I do the best I can
to listen to your breath,

to hold this monstrous thing,
beautiful,
in my mouth.

Ten Things I Want You to Do to Me

1.

Drill me out
from the hard ground.

2.

Wait on the other side
of the fence, naked
and erect.

3.

Now, now,
you'll say.
Show me where it hurts.

4.

Turn the fog lights off
and lay me on the dirt
beneath the hammock.

Lick me there.

5.

Pick at my skin
and dig into the small slit
of my navel.

6.

Hold me by the stem
in the wildflower field.

7.

Shower me
in mud-water.

8.

Cut me loose
and dump me over
the side of the ship.

9.

Watch me drown
in your chest,
in the solitude of the night.

10.

Bury me in sea salt.
Cover your eyes.

When You Get Home from Work

We leave the chicken in the oven,
the lemon and dill
on the pale cutting board.

Breadcrumbs on my hand,
I grip all of you
against your soft
stomach pouch.

You break off in my mouth,
groan.

Get me off
next to the shrimp plate
and empty beer bottles.

The Mind Wanders in Times of Despair

He throws the hot kettle at me
from across the table.

It burns.
Skin is a hot bed.

Bubbles spill;
the table is wet, hot.

The broken glass holds on
by a shard.

The hands come
and choke my neck.

He holds the hands around,
cuts off my breath.

Air, air,
where is the air?

My breasts shrivel
under the weight of his force.

He's a man, a broken man.
His hands, broken around my skin.

The water pours off the table,
down on the floor
and I can't get a towel.

The world sleeps
in a bowl of macaroni.

He's a boy, not a man.

Air, I want air.
Breathe, breathe.

Kiss me instead, my love.

Like a Goblin Fish Caught in a Net

I was tired
and my jaw clamped
down on a hand,
only to say thank you
for the heart
and the struggle.

I sang
under water,
beneath the sand.

The morning came,
and I was broken in half.

I was sold for salmon filet.

My face was hideous;
my mouth, a shotgun.

The woman that cut my belly
ripped my intestines
with her knife.

I loved once,
in pieces.

Slender Man

I met him in a forest
behind my grandmother's house.

His tentacles wrapped around me,
brought me closer
to his white face,

his smile, slender
and crooked, drunk.

I want to lick you
from inside out.

I want to do it
in front of the children
and kill you
as I burrow
into the nape
of your neck.

Do it, I say.
Stretch your slender body
against mine.

Wet me with your tears.

Stop teasing me.
Do it already.
Videotape me.

Make me the legend,
a myth, like you.

I want to become your dream.

Your Body Is a Green Dress

for sixteen-year-old Maren Sanchez
who was fatally stabbed after turning down a classmate's
request to go to prom

Your dress floats
without your body
on a boardwalk with no name.

The sleeves move in the breeze.

You're the girl
that shut the door to her room,
listened to rap
and touched herself
under the sheet,
alone.

The dress misses your skin.

The blood is gone,
wiped from your chest,
cleared from your belly.

The dress hangs in the closet
with no holes,
no breaks in the organza.

Your Love, a Broken Down Van at the Corner of Oxford and Grove

Draw a red
on its side doors.

Tell the neighbors you're stuck,
tires blown out,
doors rusted,
and handles shot
to shit.

You can't get back in.

Tell the girl on the side of the road
to stop kicking that ball at the bumper
or you'll cut her
with your pocket knife.

Take out
the useless crap in the trunk,
the used books,
and the second-hand coffee maker.

Get the lift out
and raise the car.

Jack it up high.
Electrify its misery.

If the engine starts,
you don't need me anymore.

We Are Meant to Be in the Drawer

I fell into this,
into you,
into the spaces under your skin.

I'm troubled by comparisons,
by landscapes that look the same
and different
by your ex
and her long blond hair,
her whiny voice
and whole cunt
carefully trimmed.

Dying a little each day
is better than having to face the living.

I'm castrated.
I'm inhuman,
and violently in love,
and a pussy,
a pill you pop.

I'm crazy sick by the thought of you
and her fingers wrapped around your cock.

The sun burns the top of my lip
and I'm crying
and bite the skin off with my bottom teeth,
mad that no cream will calm this.
I'm a factory of emotion,
a river that no longer exists.

I decay around my thighs
and in my thighs Christiane curls up around a phone
and waits
for me to call.

I'm the beautiful silence she's never heard,
the hard thumb after a hit to the jaw
and the hideous animal
born from jealousy
and overtaken by chains
and questions never meant for asking,
the questions that lodge
in the deepest part of the throat,
the last thing you'd want to hear me ask.

Her face is a dented car door
that hovers over me.

She's the one meant to be in the drawer
next to the sharp knives,
your back against hers.

We run this way,
and that way now,
trying to avoid suffering,

but we are alone in this,
and cry for each other on the unmade bed
next to the Bukowski book
cracked at the spine,

and your hand is on my hip
and her face is in my head

and your lips move,
and I attempt to forgive,
and you grieve,
and we forget,
and we begin
again.

The Sea Under My Bed

for A.

I reach down to pull you
out of the sea
beneath my bed,
but my hands slip
in the salt water.

I can't get to you.

I can't clasp your hand
in mine.

The water is so cold,
I get frost bite.

My arms reach
only enough to touch,
never enough to hold,
to grasp
the softness of your palm.

You stare at me
from the rough water.

I watch your face
pounded
by the spray.

I let go.

You disappear
under my bed,
far beneath the carpet.

Keep Your Moon Thoughts to Your Moon Self

Blow the moon up, a balloon,
and drag it through the air.

Stitch it with a hot needle,
drip wax on its pale stomach.

Pull its chord
and light up the sky.

Break it with a shovel.
Splatter it over gravel.

Tell the kids to cover their eyes
when it shows its teeth.

Bury it when it's white,
burn it when it's black.

Lower it into the sea,
a great white tear.

Kiss its cheek
and pray it will remember you
after it runs off in the morning.

Be the moon's half,
press your naked body into its side.

Run away with it
to a street with no name
next to a house
with closed windows.

Crack the glass
and climb out.

Wash your bloody hand
in its crater.

Wildlife in My Kitchen

It smells like fried chicken and garlic
in the kitchen
where Doris and I
watch a stinkbug
fly around the ceiling.

It bounces against the wall
and over to the long halogen lamp.

Wine stands on the glass table.

I light a cigarette
and the smoke smothers us.

The bug's wings are pretty
and make a doorbell sound.

Doris looks back at me,
her whiskers reflect the light.

She'd like to have a swipe at him,
wrestle him down from the smoky air
like the big cats
on Discovery channel.

It Takes Time

The yolk splits on the plate,
runs off the bread.

Rest your head
on the man
who will break your heart.

Love him quick.

Take the shovels
out of the garage
and bury the cat's
mangled bones.

Pull the weeds out
of the ground.

Crack
and break.

Yield your hands
from the soil.

Twist the grapes off
their stems
and smash them.

Love the cracks in your skin,
the small lines, a web
at the edge of your mouth.

Love the time
it takes for things like this
to happen: age.

Remember
when you split the egg,
slept in the atom at the center
of your mama's belly.

You split her, once
in half, too.

Play of the Duende

for Federico García Lorca

Whatever brings you here
is not real,
but indefinite and infinite space,
not with stars,
or blackness,

but something else,
quiet and dying
at the edge of the road.

It's a fish battling the hook,
or the sound of your heart
pushing an old wheelbarrow.

It might be that you are the hunter
walking through the forest,
crunching twigs and peeled bark
under your feet.

You're on the hunt
for something unknown.
You want it.

You travel to another world
filled with volcanoes under the sea,
and bathe in the lava,
let it burn its initials on you,
sweat off the old skin,

the skin that keeps imprints
of all the places you lived,
the tables where you ate,
the glasses you held
in your hand,

the empty space you've slept in,
the corner of a bedroom,

or the sky over the soaring planes,
the emptiness of cold air,

wings passing by
at five hundred miles per hour.

Staring into Space

Flowers grew like trees
high above the satellite in space.

The stars bowed their heads
in remembrance
of your birth.

You are a sun-rose
in a dark planetary garden.

I watch you orbit
away from the comfort of our house.

After one year
of staring into space,
I've lost you
in the immense distance.

The Objects

The keys,
the glasses,
the computer,
the doorknob.

I want these objects to stay,
surround me for a bit longer.

I want the glasses
perched on my nose
for one more century.

And the keys,
I want them to dangle
at the base of my hip,
and touch the keyboard
of my computer.

I want my hand to stay
wrapped around the doorknob
when I crack the door
and check
on baby Kyle sleeping.

I want the past
to stay put for now,
in the whirl of the time.

I'm not interested
in how the world began.

I want to imagine it
twenty-five billion years ago,
twenty-five billion miles away,
when I was still a star.

Words Build Homes
Inside My Head

A family lives here:
husband and wife,
two boys and a girl,
and a dog,
and a cat by the fireplace,
and a man in a face mask,
and a guy beating his head
against the wall.

Two boys become butterflies
and the girl, a butch lesbian from Brooklyn,
slicks back her hair
with a pencil comb.

The windows become a head,
the wooden frame, a rubber band
that shoots me like a bullet
inside the house
where I'm splayed on the dining room table,
my feet against a chopping block.

Out of nowhere, a dragon
burns the house down,
but keeps me cool under his wing.

The sun comes out.

The house is burnt to a crisp
and I look away,

down the block paved with commas
and periods and lots of semicolons,
a couple of vowels perched on trees.

The words come together,
I can almost see them.

The Wine

Imagine yourself taller,
thinner,
happier.

The wine makes it happen,

a magic trick that works,
but only you know it.

Close your eyes
when you spin
on the carousel ride,

swirling around
and around,
passing kisses through the air,
your hair blowing behind you,
knotting up in clumps

before you wake up
on someone else's couch,
two days later.

The Beds I Slept In

The world is strewn with beds
I slept in,
like marks on my skin,
scattered in cities and countries,
in Hiltons
and Holiday Inns.

I slept in all these rooms
with people I knew
and didn't,
fucked or made love to,
or just slept,
backs against backs
against the bed sheets.

Beds, long and short,
king and queen,
double, single,
together, alone,

again and again,
eight hours a day
in a bed,
not knowing
where I was
with you, or her,
or him,

or in a dream,
dreaming of the bed,
dreaming of me.

But it's not a bed at all.
It's a place lost in the matrix
of soft and hard bodies
crushed with breakups,
breakthroughs,
and people our beds don't know.

We cheat on our beds
with other beds,
never say we're sorry.

We cry, sob, and sleep
in the fetal position,
take shelter in pillows,
taking for granted
the thread count,
the box spring,

the bed's open palm
holding us.

Black & White Kiss by the Hotel de Ville

for Robert Doisneau

Their clothes blow in the wind
and wrap in the bend of their backs.

They hang on the wall over my four-poster bed,
necks stretch out to kiss each other.

Around them, people walk
on tiger lilies.

Their mouths,
a cave where they hide
and sleep next to hungry bears.

The world is colorless.

I spread my limbs out
as if I'm a cross
they hang themselves on.

They die kissing
for me.

The Mudslide

for the survivors and victims of the Oso mudslide

Concrete crumbles;
stone washes away.

The house curls into the pond
and chips.

Rubber ducks drown
in an empty parking lot,
and sheet rock wraps the road
with its warped belly.

Mud, a smile
that consumes the slanted highway.

The town is full
of the presence of people
who have sunk beneath the dirt,

their tiny hairs,
lost fibers in the wind.

We Are Already Ghosts

Dying is safe.

We all do it.

No more asking,
just knowing.

No miracles,
only design by nature.

No mistakes,
only footprints
and pebbles on the road.

We aren't who
we thought we were.

The Candy Bombers

for Gail S. "Hal" Halvorsen

We are the squadron
that dropped candy
from the sky,

covered the ground in mints
and chewing gum.

They carted the children away,
bellies full of cracked corn,

teeth rotted
and broken,

mouths splintered
with salt sticks.

Their parents paid
for a place on the wagon

and watched the sugar fall
like snowflakes from the sky.

Hard Bread and Beans

I step into the dirt.
Its dampness
makes me feel
I exist.

I'm at home here,
in the middle of blinking bugs,

with a campfire,
some hard bread
and beans.

Keep Smiling

On nights like this,
the road bends into blackness
and the white lines
paved into the tar
look like slivers of bone,
and the air whistles through
the open window,
and the trees rustle their feathers
and music lights up like stars,
loud stars.

The seat is warm from your jeans
and the smile on your face
feels like the first time
you've ever smiled.
It feels good,
so good that you keep smiling,
you hold it there,
that crooked smile
and stare in front of you
through the windshield.

You look through the night
towards something you see,
and you recognize it
in front of you,
like when you recognize
someone you know
and you stare,

and smile,
and drive past him,

passing through him,
and he into you,

and the night passes
through both of you.

You smoke your last cigarette,
share a light with the wind,
and the wind whistles
as you drive.

Acknowledgments

The author wishes to acknowledge the editors of the following magazines, anthologies, and journals where these poems originally appeared:

Drunken Boat: "Love Poem"

Blue Lake Review: "Your Love, a Broken Van at the Corner of Oxford and Grove"

Narrative Northeast: "Keep Smiling"

Poetry Boston: "Breakable Things," "Play of the Duende," and "Words Build Homes Inside My Head"

Domestic Cherry: "First-date Oysters" and "Traditional"

I'd also like to give a special thank you and acknowledgment to Claudia Serea, my wonderfully talented editor, poet, and dear friend, who gave her time and advice to shape *Breakable Things* as well as my previous collection, *The Dark Cave Between My Ribs*.

Notes

The Slender Man: (also known as Slenderman) is a fictional character that originated as an Internet meme created by Something Awful forums user Eric Knudsen (a.k.a. "Victor Surge") in 2009. It is depicted as resembling a thin, unnaturally tall man with a blank and usually featureless face, wearing a black suit. Stories of the Slender Man commonly feature him stalking, abducting, or traumatizing people, particularly children. The Slender Man is not confined to a single narrative, but appears in many disparate works of fiction, mostly composed online (Wikipedia, Slender Man).

The Play of the Duende: In Federico Garcia-Lorca's acclaimed essay, "Play and Theory of the Duende" (1933), Duende is defined as one of three incarnations of artistic inspiration, rousing human creativity. In the essay, Lorca identifies three distinct spiritual entities that inspire all human creativity: 1). muses, 2). angels, and 3). the duende. As the essay progresses, Lorca defines and compares each of these supernatural art-inducing dynamos (http://www.duendeart.org).

Black & White Kiss: Robert Doisneau (1912-1994) is one of the most famous French photographers. His photographs were of common people, in common situations, often in the streets of Paris. *Kiss by the Hotel de Ville* is arguably one of his most famous photographs (Jen Tarara).

The Candy Bombers: Colonel Gail S. "Hal" Halvorsen (born October 10, 1920) is a retired career officer and command pilot in the United States Air Force known as the original Candy Bomber or the "Rosinenbomber" in Germany. Shortly before landing at the Berlin Tempelhof Airport in the American sector of Berlin, Halvorsen would drop candy attached to parachutes to children below. This action, which was dubbed Operation Little Vittlesand sparked similar efforts by other crews, was the source of the popular name for the pilots: the candy bombers. Halvorsen wanted to help raise the morale of the children during the time of uncertainty and privation (Wikipedia, Gail Halvorsen).

He Breaks Me Like a Glass Plate: "I'm so tired, so tired. I'm so tired, I wish I was the moon tonight." From the Neko Case song "I Wish I Was the Moon Tonight."

About the Author

Loren Kleinman is a young, American-born poet with roots in New Jersey. Her poetry explores the results of love and loss, and how both themes affect an individual's internal and external voice. Loren has a BA in English Literature from Drew University and an MA in Creative and Critical Writing from the University of Sussex (UK). She was the recipient of the Spire Press Poetry Prize (2003), was a 2000 and 2003 Pushcart Prize nominee, and was a 2004 Nimrod/Pablo Neruda Prize finalist for poetry. Loren is also a columnist for IndieReader. com where she interviews New York Times bestselling indie authors.

Follow Loren:
lorenkleinman.com
twitter.com/LorenKleinman
facebook.com/lorenkleinman